God's Carnal Children
and The Word of God
An Extension of the Book 'Traversing Babylon'

Peter W. Rouzaud

To Muriel Langley:
'As a mother, continually showing Christ's character through
her example and encouragement.'

•

To Marvie Toma:
'Who was the first who taught me
how to react to the idea of a vindictive God.'

For the sake of clarity, all references to The Church, invisible
and universal are spelled with a capital 'C'. While organizations
and local fellowships are not.

"For we know that the law is spiritual, but I am carnal, sold under sin." Rom.7.14

"For when one says, "I am of Paul," and another, "I am of Apollos," are you not carnal?" 1Cor.3.4

Cover Painting: 'David and Goliath'
By Tiziano Vecellio (1477-1576)

Preface

This book came out of the need to clarify some thoughts, and answer some obvious (and legitimate) questions raised in the book before it, 'Traversing Babylon.' Rather than writing the entire book again, or including a lengthy appendix, I chose to write this book, which I thought, could stand on its own.

Naturally, there are some repetitious thoughts, but I concluded there is enough difference in the subject, and partial answers just provoke more questions, so here it is.

The conclusions in this book, I think, is key to understanding, and answering, the many accusations non-Christians throw at believers. Correcting our understanding of Scripture also goes a long way to remedy all the questions about "contradictions," and "historical inaccuracies," both in Christianity and Jewish tradition.

Another advantage to the hypothesis presented here, Christianity will no longer take the place of Jesus being a stumbling block. In other words, Jesus Himself, as prophesied, is the stumbling block (Rom.9.33), but some honest seekers cannot even come close to hearing about Jesus because there is so much background noise among the people who claim to speak for God. Things like: "You have to believe what the Bible says about creation." Or, "You must believe in a literal....., etc."

How many seekers want to meet our loving God, but cannot hear above so much confusion implying we must believe the Bible's record on all points.

> *"For this is good and acceptable in the sight of God our Savior, who desires all men to be saved and to come to the knowledge of the truth.*
>
> *For there is one God and **one Mediator** between God and men, the Man Christ Jesus," 1Tim.2.3-5*

What if you could believe, that for multiple centuries, mankind was like the children in the book, 'Lord of the Flies.' The world and the Hebrews were like tribes of children marooned on the island of earth, attempting to please an invisible and unknowable God. When God tried to reach our ant-like brains, we amalgamated what He said into our vulgar, coarse, and idolatrous thinking.

Alas, God had to do something drastic; He manifested Himself into a man; that Man was the divine expression, the true reliable picture of God, our mediator, the only Begotten Son of God.

Ever since Jesus walked this earth, religious systems keep falling back into that barbaric, Old Testament understanding of God.

The difference now is, Jesus has left us with a Comforter, The Paraclete, God in us, Who is continually reminding us how our Father is. One aim of this book is to provoke you to listen to our Comforter above all else.

Table of Contents

Introduction

My wife and I began our pilgrim's journey in 1969 with our conversion during the Jesus movement. We fell totally in love with the person of Jesus Christ, and we love Him just as much today. When I began, I picked up my Bible, and I did not put it down. First I started carrying a large Bible wherever I went. Then I got a pocket edition of the whole Bible with print so small I could barely read it. In my forties, my eyes got so bad I had to give that Bible up and kept a larger print Bible in my car. Now, with these smart phones, I again carry the Bible with me at all times. I believed, as I still do, the Bible is inspired by God; and with it, I can better become like Jesus.

During my early years as a Christian, a preacher I respected once told me, "there are few who will follow Jesus whithersoever He leads." In my mind, I vowed, "I would be the one who would." I was thinking about being tortured for Christ, or going on the mission field, or defying my unbelieving family. When one is young it is easy to make vows; we throw them around in our zeal the same way a first week Marine thinks he is ready for war. When I made that vow, I had not even considered; I might have to sacrifice what I had become, my identity as a Christian.

To begin, I would like to tell you a story. It is a true story. However, it involves the miraculous, and you may have a hard time believing it. If you do not, the story may still be appreciated as an allegory, the particulars are unnecessary for my point:

Ever since my conversion, I have been good at arguing a point. I considered apologetics as part of my "ministry." One day I ran into an acquaintance of mine who was of another faith. Because we both loved a good Biblical sparring match, we got into it. He brought up an explanation for a verse and point I had not considered. I knew the verse well, but the more I pondered it, the more valid his argument became. I was stumped like I had never been before.

The point the man was making, if true, changed the entire representation of who Jesus is - He would no longer be God. The more I thought about it, the more confused I became. "Had I spent so many years following only a man, but calling Him God?"

As I was earnestly considering these things, God spoke to me, "Peter, would you convert to this man's religion if I asked you to?"

So, you think, 'Of course, I will follow God's leading no matter where He takes me.' It is not so easy when it comes down to it. You see, I was an elder in my church, I was respected in my family as a spiritually solid and dependable person. Being an independent contractor most of my business contacts were the same faith as myself. I was currently teaching Bible study and was respected for convictions I had maintained and the answers I was able to give. Besides this, this particular religion I was being asked to consider, in my mind, was one of the worst possible options. On and on, the cost of my re-conversion was starting to mount.

You see, when God speaks to you, it is like a two-edged sword, God was using his Word to separate what is true faith in Him, or in the systems I had adopted.

The more I thought, the more I became aware, the cost of this change would be too much to answer easily.

After some hours of consideration, I answered God, "OK Father, I will do it if this is where you are leading me, I am willing re-convert."

At that very moment, there flashed in my mind the answer to the question that had me stumped! It was easy; "why hadn't I seen it before?" So God finally said, "you do not have to re-convert, I just wanted all your life."

God has since asked some hard things of me; some without the same happy ending. I've gone through some similar consequences I was worried about when God led me through that test so many years ago.

I should note, God speaking so plainly is not a common occurrence. I can count on one hand how many times God's voice was so unambiguous.

As you read this book, please know, I still love my Bible, I still believe it to be inspired; However, it is no longer on equal footing and replacement for God's Word; it is no longer His voice. Furthermore, I don't believe the words in the Bible always reflect God's heart, but His heart can be found there.

Consequently, the study of scripture is much harder for me now, the scriptures are not stepped instructions, rules, proof texts, which should be memorized; they are not even "a handbook for life."

I see the Bible as God's gift to me. However, I must do the work of a Berean, pray while I read it, and attempt to hear God's voice, His Word; to understand His person, He who is "without variableness, neither shadow of turning." I must sort through the clutter and scribbles of man's many carnal representations of God to actually find Him.

If you care to read on, perhaps you too will find, God is much better than you ever thought He was. I hope you will find; the hypothesis advanced in these pages will give you an answer for why the God of your experience, the one who has shown you boundless mercies, is different from the God depicted in the Old Testament.

My Definitions and Note

Carnal: *Our Flesh; That part of us which is nonredeemable, that part which is always in conflict with The Holy Spirit.*

Inspiration: *God Breathed into the ear of man*

The Word: *Divine Expression; Logos*

Scripture: *A document, i.e. Holy Writ, or man's understanding and writing about, or transcribing what he believed to be 'Divine Expression'.*

I recently read, that while in our mother's womb babies are completely sterile. But after a short stay in the hospital. After the baby is handled by doctors, nurses, parents, and relatives. And after the child's skin is exposed to sheets and blankets, and the air of this world; by the time that baby leaves the hospital the microbes that now inhabit its body, both inside and out, far outnumber the cells in its own body. Those microbes will stay with that baby throughout its entire life. Some of these microbes do good, many are bad.

Have you ever tried to touch your glasses without leaving a mark? This is the nature of the 'carnal' (as the Spanish say, carne - flesh). We are 'carnal' and everywhere we go, we leave an imprint. Everything we touch cannot escape from being affected by us.

"Jesus said to him, "He who is bathed needs only to wash his feet, but is completely clean; and you are clean,....." Jn.13.10(a)

This was Jesus answer to Peter when Peter wanted Jesus to 'wash his whole body' (Jn.13.9). I hope you see the allegory of the microbes because it is not only true of our bodies, but it is also true, as Jesus implied, of our minds and souls. Every person who has ever taught you; every influence from your past, the culture you live in, and your own behavior, has some effect on your carnal mind and the disposition of your soul. As a first generation believer, I can tell you how hard it is to undo the massive influence of the sins of my youth, and all the sinful lives who had touched me. Many of these influences are like microbes carrying diseases, which God in all His omnipotence is unable to heal; until our death. If you believe otherwise, you are kidding yourself.

There is only one person who was able to escape this reality.

This is how it has always been; this is as it will always be; until that day when we leave our flesh behind and "we are caught up together to meet the Lord in the air." (1Thes.4.17)

Carnal Heroes

Everyone has heroes. Sports fans, science fans, political fans, preacher fans; everyone has someone they admire. Unconsciously our heroes are thought to be without the failings *we* experience. We feel they have arrived and the things which make us fail do not apply to them. They are in a place we aspire to be.

Let's look at some of our Bible heroes:

*"Jacob said to his father, "**I am Esau** your firstborn; I have done just as you told me; please arise, sit and eat of my game, that your soul may bless me." Gen.27.19*

"Now Samson went to Gaza and saw a harlot there, and went in to her." Jug.16.1

"But it displeased Jonah exceedingly, and he became angry. So he prayed to the LORD, and said, "Ah, LORD, was not this what I said when I was still in my country? Therefore I fled previously to Tarshish; for I know that You are a gracious and

merciful God, slow to anger and abundant in lovingkindness, One who relents from doing harm." Jonah 4.1-2

"Then it happened one evening that David arose from his bed and walked on the roof of the king's house. And from the roof he saw a woman bathing, and the woman was very beautiful to behold. So David sent and inquired about the woman. And someone said, "Is this not Bathsheba, the daughter of Eliam, the wife of Uriah the Hittite?" 2Sam.11.2-3

"Now when Peter had come to Antioch, I withstood him to his face, because he was to be blamed;..." Gal.2.11

"When after some days Paul said to Barnabas, "Let us now go back and visit our brethren in every city where we have preached the word of the Lord, and see how they are doing. Now Barnabas was determined to take with them John called Mark. But Paul insisted that they should not take with them the one who had departed from them in

Pamphylia, and had not gone with them to the work. Then the contention became so sharp that they parted from one another. And so Barnabas took Mark and sailed to Cyprus;" Act.15.36-39

An adolescent dreaming of the perfect spouse will never imagine them with a blemish. Likewise, we like our heroes to be without spot or blemish. Everything about their character should be perfection. These are only fanciful dreams. In reality, we all carry with us characteristics which are part of our humanity- our flesh, the 'carnal' part of our minds and bodies. Your Bible heroes were no exception to this.

Because our flesh is inherently selfish, we are prone to the immoral. Immorality is the acting out of our choices when someone, others or myself, become hurt in some way. The Christian would call this "sin."

By itself, our 'flesh' is not immoral. Our flesh is neither moral nor immoral until we make our choices. Though the flesh is the animal side of us, it is no more immoral/moral than our computer; It is non-moral. Again, because of our instinct for self-survival, the flesh carries with it a desire for self, including power and dominance over others for our own benefit.

"And the LORD God formed man of the dust of the ground, and breathed into his nostrils the breath of life; and man became a living being." Gen.2.7

The one and only difference between humans and the rest of the animal kingdom is the 'breath of God' within us. With this 'image' there is a type of sovereignty, a self-will, a self-consciousness, an "I am that I am." We have an awareness of ourselves the rest of the animal kingdom does not share.

However, because the flesh is instinctively selfish, it cannot be subject to God. For the Christian, this means it must be controlled by keeping what we see as carnal, on a cross. (Gal.2.20)

"Because the carnal mind is enmity against God; for it is not subject to the law of God, nor indeed can be." Rom.8.7

After conversion, the Christian becomes acutely aware the conflicts there are with the instinctual/flesh side of us. Paul speaks to this in Romans chapter 7. Of which we will speak some later.

Romans 7 indicates, the animal part of us, the carnal, cannot be converted, it can only be overcome. However, 'overcome' as we might, the mind of the flesh is continually running interference where the Holy Spirit is attempting to lead. If you give this hypothesis some thought, you will see why our heroes made so many mistakes. Just as you and I make so many mistakes- in marriage, life, and ministry, so did our Bible heroes.

After conversion, the Christian becomes acutely aware the conflicts there are with the instinctual/flesh side of us. Paul speaks to this in Romans chapter 7. Of which we will speak some later.

Romans 7 indicates, the animal part of us, the carnal, cannot be converted, it can only be overcome. However, 'overcome' as Christianity's detractors love to point out the mistakes of people of the Bible: and they are often right. These believe they have the perfect argument against the scriptures, and they do, so long as we insist 'the Bible in its entirety, represents the Person and perfection of God.' However, when we admit 'the carnality of man had, and has, something to do with life and ministry; as well as his understanding of God', those tools of Christianity's enemies are taken away. It is only when we insist on something false that our enemies have us trapped.

I've had scores of debates with unbelievers about the Bible, and before my present convictions, I would argue somewhat convincingly about the veracity of Scripture.

I have to confess; I used my adversaries ignorance to my advantage. Whenever I would challenge my opponents to prove their claims that the Bible "is full of contradictions," they never could provide evidence. I look back on this now with some shame; and I am wholly convinced, 'apologetics' has almost no value for the Kingdom of God. But this is not my point; my point is, the Bible does have some huge issues. And jut because someone can artfully propose answers, does not solve the blinding truth of these matters.

Without getting into the arguments about 'contradictions,' I believe the image we represent of our God is the most important issue of all. I hope by the end of this book you will see; contradictions are of little consequence when we consider how much our loving God is maligned, and often because of His children.

God Chooses Imperfect People

Did you note the scriptures I began with? The Bible is full of stories describing, in painful detail, the carnal humanity God has chosen for His work and inheritance. As far back as the Patriarchs God has used ordinary and sinful humans. We like to think of Moses as that powerful figure we see in the movies, but we often forget he was actually insecure and humble (Ex.4.10-17). Then there are people like Gideon, who did great things as well, but started out as an ordinary man; fearful, doubting and needing gentle reassurance.

> *"For the eyes of the Lord move to and fro throughout the earth so that He may support those whose heart is completely His....." 2Ch.16,9a (Amplified Bible)*

Unconsciously Christians overlook the genuine humanity of our Bible heroes. We look at ourselves compared to the deeds they have done, and feel they must have been supermen; the opposite is true.

So men are less likely to glorify themselves, God prefers to choose men and women who are weak and flawed. People who have 'issues,' individuals who are not strong in themselves. These are the best candidates for His work. This is a theme running throughout the Bible, from the beginning of the Old Testament and throughout the New.

Some of God's servants have some serious faults; cheating, like Jacob; a weakness for women, like King David and Samson; unmerciful and self-willed like Jonah. The Bible records the failings of heroes and the chaos affecting the people they served. Nonetheless, indefectibility is not the criteria for service to God.

When God chooses His servants, the only thing required is faith. And that 'faith' may not even be the variety that produces unquestioned obedience; Moses and Jonah prove this. The only thing needed is a heart wanting God. Perfection, or absolute obedience, if possible, comes later- if ever.

There are (at least) two facets of faith:

"But without faith it is impossible to please Him, for he who comes to God must believe that He is, and that He is a rewarder of those who diligently seek Him." Heb.11.6

You may think this verse is a stretch to show my point (it possibly is). But I believe you can see both facets here. Regardless, the experiences of Patriarchs and Saints prove this to be the case: There is a faith where you believe "God Is"; and there is a faith that believes, "He is a rewarder of those of diligently seek Him." In my view, it is possible to come to know God, and be imperfect and not seek Him, or obey Him; like Samson. However, God still may choose us for some task. Incredibly, this is the way Balaam was too.

It is the residing faith in our hearts which determines our relationship with God. This is the type of faith which answers God's call to us. This was true for the Old Testament believers, and it also applies to the New Testament in Christ. A man or women may have nothing to offer God, but God takes us with all our imperfections.

> *"And His name, through faith in His name, has made this man strong, whom you see and know. Yes, the faith which comes through Him has given him this perfect soundness in the presence of you all."*
> *Ac.3.16*

"But now the righteousness of God apart from the law is revealed, being witnessed by the Law and the Prophets, even the righteousness of God, through faith in Jesus Christ, to all and on all who believe. For there is no difference;" Rom.3.21-22

Responding to God's call is only the initiation of God's pleasure with us. It is our obedience to God which further 'pleases Him.' Faith in Christ and what He has done is the deciding factor whether I belong to the family of God. Our natural lives demonstrate this; it is possible to have relatives, a sibling, a child, we have no pleasure in, and yet we have a relationship of love. On this same basis, we have membership in the family of God. Service, and obedience, as Jonah has shown us - our pleasing God, often comes later.

So you see because the heroes in the Old Testament were just like you and me, there are countless reasons they made mistakes about who God was, and what He expected of them.

The Carnal Tools of Administrations and Operations

"No one can serve two masters; for either he will hate the one and love the other, or else he will be loyal to the one and despise the other. You cannot serve God and mammon." Mat.6.24

"And I say to you, make friends for yourselves by unrighteous mammon, that when you fail, they may receive you into an everlasting home." Lu.16.9

"For the love of money is a root of all kinds of evil, for which some have strayed from the faith in their greediness, and pierced themselves through with many sorrows." 1Tim.6.10

Of all the inventions of man, and of all the tools used by churches, money tops the list as the most dangerous. When we have problems of any type we unconsciously hope for money that it will remedy our problems; consequently mammon becomes like a God to us.

*"A feast is made for laughter, And wine makes merry; **But money answers everything**." Ecc.10.19*

The early Church had humble beginnings, they met in houses, poverty was everywhere, so the Church shared everything. As time went on the Church began to organize. Soon after organizing, money became an integral part of the operations of churches. Apparently, God is okay with this. All but a few Christians hate what money brings to the Church. However, even though God certainly allows money to be part of the church, and the operations of our lives, it brings with it many hazards. Not only does God permit the use of this carnal tool, as the scripture indicates, but He also encourages the wise use of it. (Lu.16.9).

However simple life was for the early Church, church life has now evolved into a chaos of sectarianism, Schools of Simony, advertising, pledge drives, gimmicks, and professionalism. Even with all these carnal tools, still, God has advanced His Church.

The problems which money brings into the Church is undeniable. There are, however, tools man brings into

God's work which is more subtle but still undermine God's model in the New Testament.

> *But the thing displeased Samuel when they said, "Give us a king to judge us." So Samuel prayed to the LORD. And the LORD said to Samuel, "Heed the voice of the people in all that they say to you; for they have not rejected you, but they have rejected Me, that I should not reign over them."* 1Sam.8.6-7

Many churches make choices like Israel wanting a king. Samuel spells out the consequences of taking a king, and God compares Israel's desires, to serving other gods after coming out of Egypt. As with money, men administrate the church outside the patterns of inspired scripture. Similar to Israel, churches are, in a sense, rejecting God, and copying the carnal administrations of the world. Instead of allowing God to work, churches have chosen carnal means to control church life. As a consequence, just about everything in a church revolves around the question of available funds to acquire professional results. Churches, like individuals, fall into the trap where they unconsciously believe money (not God) is the source of their help (Ecc.10.19).

Just because God gives His Church broad leniency to administrate His flock, just as He was with Israel wanting a king, does not mean He is happy with man's choices. Amazingly, Jesus still said, 'The gates of hell will not prevail against His Church"! We should not confuse God's endorsement with His longsuffering.

Let me give you a personal example, and what follows is as Paul said, "boasting in the Lord": The night my wife and I accepted Jesus as savior, a well-known Pastor in our area was the guest preacher. We raised our hands to 'accept Christ,' and we have never looked back. We have been continually faithful to one another, and to the Lord. We were miraculously saved from an utterly lost condition. Apparently, the seed of God's Word 'fell on good soil'. However, some years after my wife and I were converted, we discovered that same pastor, the very one who preached the night of our conversion, had been involved in a long time affair, coincident with our conversion. Now I ask you, was this pastor's imperfections limiting God's work in our lives? Actually, a better question, 'Does the fruit of my family's life proves this man was faithful to the Lord'?

God, as He did with King David, continues to use carnal mankind.

Certainly, there is a line where the Holy Spirit becomes grieved with churches and people. When this line is crossed, there is no longer any anointing from God. Even though a church may say they represent Jesus Christ, God can no longer use that corporate body; there ceases to be real light there. (Rev.2.5) But we cannot always be sure when this happens.

Such is the blindness of those who claim God's endorsement, church organizations can become imperialistic, taking over whole continents in the name of God; use genocide, torture and burn dissenters to death on a smoldering fire, and still claim they represent God! With these as the exception, God is incredibly tolerant of those who claim to speak for Him. And just as incredible, even among the most detestable groups, there are *individuals* whom God claims as His children. Oh, the mercy and longsuffering of God!

Does this mean God does not have a preferred method of operation? No, I don't think God's acceptance of our carnal tools means that at all. In fact, it may be part of the entire process where God determines the quality of our service.

Besides this, we can be certain, our variety of Christianity, even if 100% of God's pattern, will be carnal in some way. The Apostle Paul spoke the following of himself, and all work of churches.

"For we know in part and we prophesy in part.."
    1Cor.13.9

Like all of us today, the Apostle Paul saw himself *in process*. In fact, as I have already shown with the Apostle Paul correcting (the great Holy Spirit-filled leader of the Church), Peter. This demonstrates, there were human vulnerabilities even among those who, not only walked with Jesus but had been in the faith for some years. Does this diminish Peter as an Apostle? Absolutely not, this is the average human condition.

God is satisfied with allowing ordinary human beings run His operations - but only so long as they love Him and are walking in faith. There is only one test of genuine adoption of God- if the believer honors the Son of God who has come in the flesh, (1Jn.4.2.) All other tests (there are dozens) in 1John, are extensions of the same or relating to the quality of our faith. These are measures to judge ourselves, not to nitpick the faith of another. Even in 1st John, our Lord's words, 'Judge not,' still apply. Whom God has accepted into His fold, we have no business rejecting. And He has accepted some real oddballs. But being an odd-ball does not determine if a person has encountered God.

I've come to discover; God can use a child to speak to me. If He can use a donkey (Num.22.28) to talk to a man, He can certainly use that man who smells as he's hadn't taken a bath in weeks; or that woman who talks too much in church. "God has chosen the foolish things of the world to shame the wise" (1Cor.1.27), is not only speaking of the wise of the world, but it also applies to the wise in churches as well. Be wary, since God specializes in humbling the proud. That person who you think has no right to correct you, and God may still use.

As much as we would like to think the authors of the Bible to be perfect, this is clearly not the case. These were men who were not unlike us.

The Scripture is no different than any other thing, or person God has given His people; all things are partial and eventually dissolved when that which is perfect comes.

We must face the facts of how the scripture has come to us; it came through sinful men. There are many authors of the sixty-six books of the Protestant Bible. No one is sure how many, perhaps 35 or 40+. To say that every word in the Bible is in every sense perfect and factual, and wholly represents God's heart, would be a miracle beyond the parting of the Red Sea.

Of course, finding the scripture perfect is desirable. How much easier it would be to let our brains go into neutral and solemnly declare, 'the earth, the stars and galaxies, all of life and matter, had no beginning until about 7000 years ago'. And mankind roamed, and probably fought Tyrannosaurus Rex for food'. And how simple to explain the light from distant galaxies, or even the closest star, Alpha Centauri (4.367 light years away), appeared on earth instantly. (Yet, we would say, 'ridiculous' if we heard such answers from Christianity's adversaries.)

In its simple, straightforward and legalistic way, Fundamentalism has an appeal. One only believes church tradition and doctrine; everything about life and activity is dictated, 'don't do these..; but do these two or three times a week'. And if you should slip up, one only has to perform the dictated acts of penance. No thought, no study, no questions, and surely no dissent; just attend and believe what you are told. If anyone asks you a hard question, just refer him or her to the person paid to answer, and protect was has been established as truth.

All organized religion, more or less, operate in this way. If any might suggest any answer outside a prescribed set of beliefs, they are not welcome. Such faith is not faith in God, but in the original story tellers of the Bible. This type of faith gives the Christian some peace; but as I see it, it is peace of the wrong sort. Our peace should not come from a quixotic view of faith in the Bible, but rather a faith in the goodness of God.

Furthermore, we see in the Bible itself, how vulnerable the fathers of our faith were. Consider one of

David's prayers, a sample of Psalm 109, and many expressions like this in the Bible.

> "In return for my love they are my accusers, But I give myself to prayer. Thus they have rewarded me evil for good, And hatred for my love. Set a wicked man over him, And let an accuser stand at his right hand. When he is judged, let him be found guilty, And let his prayer become sin. Let his days be few, And let another take his office Let his children be fatherless, And his wife a widow. Let his children continually be vagabonds, and beg; Let them seek their bread also from their desolate places. Let the creditor seize all that he has, And let strangers plunder his labor. Let there be none to extend mercy to him, Nor let there be any to favor his fatherless children. Let his posterity be cut off, And in the generation following let their name be blotted out. Let the iniquity of his fathers be remembered before the LORD, And let not the sin of his mother be blotted out. Let them be continually before the LORD, That He may cut off the memory of them from the earth;......" Ps.109.5-14 (only a portion of the curses!)

Because David was a man after God's heart (Ac.13.22), Bible teachers try to explain these curses as if they somehow reflects God's righteous judgment on sinful man; that without God's grace, we and our children, all deserve these curses. What follows is what Charles Spurgeon said:

> *"We confess that as we read some of these verses we have need of all our faith and reverence to accept them as the voice of inspiration; but the exercise is good for the soul, for it educates our sense of ignorance, and tests our teachableness. Yes, Divine Spirit, we can **and do believe that even these dread words from which we shrink have a meaning consistent with the attributes of the Judge of all the earth, though his name is LOVE**. How this may be we shall know hereafter." Charles Spurgeon*

As much as I love and respect Charles Spurgeon's work, this makes no sense; love loses all meaning if we attribute this Psalm to the actual character of God. These expressions of David no more reflect the heart of God than the psalmist's adultery with Bathsheba.

Spurgeon and others are merely rejecting reason for the sake of dogma; that inspiration means the words on the Bible's pages always reflect God's heart.

So, what is the meaning of Psalm 109? The explanation is simple; David prayed with complete honesty to God. He was utterly transparent with God. He prayed what he was feeling, and it is recorded in scripture. His words are part of the carnality of mankind. The Holy Spirit has given us this psalm for the same reason He has given us these similar words:

> *"O daughter of Babylon, who are to be destroyed, Happy the one who repays you as you have served us! Happy the one who takes and dashes Your little ones against the rock!" Ps.137:8-9*

This psalm leaves us utterly exposed. This is how men feel in war; after they have lost everything. This is what they become, but it is a grave error to teach these things the psalmist speaks as if they are a reflection of God's heart and holiness.

The inspired Word of God includes, as James spoke, Elijah, a man with a nature like ours, (KJV, "Passions"). When James said this, he was not speaking of the passions of the Holy Spirit, but that which is carnal (human) in us; Yet, still God hears, and responds to His children. (Ja.5.17) However, God will not answer a prayer which is outside of His nature or outside of His will (Ja.4.2-3). Elijah praying for rain is one thing, but praying for the death of a man and the total ruin of his family, is another (Ps.109)

How often is, He whose name is 'Wonderful Counselor, The Prince of Peace' (Is.9.6), misjudged, and maligned because Christians insist every word in the Bible somehow reflects some attribute of God? How often is the beautiful name of Jesus blasphemed, because Christians are stubbornly ignorant how God used carnal men to write the Bible?

We do not have to take the position, that all scripture reflect God's attributes, to still believe the Bible to be inspired. If we do, we get ourselves into all kinds of theological troubles. Take, for instance, extreme "Christians" who stand on the street corners and declare how 'God hates homosexuals.' One group extends this logic, proclaiming, 'God sent a mass murderer, killing fifty in a nightclub to exercise His judgment on the gay lifestyle". In some ways, this 'church' is more honest than most Christians, who believe this act was an atrocity.

If we can believe God never changes, and He sent His people to wipe out several cities in Canaan, including children, why should we not think God may instruct one of His servants to do this in this present age? And when I bring up the question to my veteran friends and suggest Jesus would not want Christians to advance their temporal nationalistic agendas through war; almost all argue from the point of the Old Testament stories, saying; "God endorsed, even commanded war after the exodus of Israel."

If we are to be consistent, we can with all honesty reinforce our militancy, kill in the name of God, even innocent children, while salving our consciences with Old Testament passages. "Why should we not duplicate Old Testament examples if we have faith in the God of the inerrant Bible; and the authority of scripture?"

Certainly, you must see, this is not faith in God, but faith in the ones who brought us the stories in the first place.

Ascribing Man's Nature to God

There are many verses, whole chapters, even whole books, where the carnal activities of man are recorded and alleged to be God's instructions. In every ancient culture with their propensity to violence, the gods of these cultures become extensions of man's morals, culture and nature. I believe Israel, coming out of Egypt and forward, were not exceptions. I contend that Jehovah God was (and is) nothing like the gods of those ancient cultures. Nor was He, or is He anything like Israel thought Him to be. Again, the story of Jericho:

> *"And they utterly destroyed all that was in the city, both man and woman, young and old, ox and sheep and donkey, with the edge of the sword."* Josh.6.21

How do we cope with scriptures like this?

> *"These six things **the LORD hates**, Yes, seven are an abomination to Him: A proud look, A lying tongue, **Hands that shed innocent blood**,"* Prov.6.16-17

Which is it? Were the works of Joshua representing God; or do the words of Prov.6.17 represent Him? Would God command us to do what He hates? Would He also tell us to lie, or to be proud, or as this proverb goes on to say, would He instruct us to devise an evil plan? We must choose which of these verses represent God's character; both cannot.

Think about it for a moment: Did God embrace Moses and later the Children of Israel because they had a perfect understanding of Jehovah?

Remember, Moses had no idea who was talking to him from the 'burning bush':

> *"Then Moses said to God, "Indeed, when I come to the children of Israel and say to them, 'The God of your fathers has sent me to you,' and they say to me, 'What is His name?' what shall I say to them?"*
> *Ex.3.13*

God began to educate Moses about whom Moses was speaking to. Up to this point, going back to the early patriarchs, God's identity was a complete mystery. God did not have a name, neither was there any written law. As Israel gradually separated themselves from the god's of their surrounding neighbors, we can naturally surmise they had some wrong ideas about the nature of God. Since the Person of Jehovah God was new to the Israelite's, we can assume they imagined Him to be someone entirely different than what is shown us in the New Testament. Remember, Israel had been in Egypt for four hundred years. Not only was God obscure before their arrival to Egypt, but He also began to be wholly compromised after that amount of time in Egypt.

In addition, there is a theory, with some evidence, Pharaoh Akhenaton [Amenhotep] was the Pharaoh of Joseph. As far as we know Akhenaton was the sole Monotheist in Ancient Egypt's history. No one really knows how he arrived at his beliefs. Was he influenced by Joseph, and amalgamated Joseph's God into his belief system? Because the one true God was so undefined; and since Jehovah God had not been identified as yet. Prior to the giving of the Law God could be imagined, and be believed to be anything, even a calf. (Ex.32.22-24)

Any study of the Patriarchs will show you, none of them had any sort of understanding who God actually was. From Joseph's perspective, God could have been 'Aten.'

This is not so far-fetched; remember the story of Jacob's wife, Rachel, Joseph's mother. How she lied to Laban, her father, when she stole his gods. (Gen.31.34)

I know this idea sounds odd to most Christians, this is because most assume God chose Moses, Joshua, and most of Israel's early leaders, because they were excellent men, and had some great and righteous behavior; or perhaps some special insight into Jehovah God. Nothing is further from the truth. As Christianity rightly teaches, God has always chosen us by His grace, through faith. This is constant throughout both Testaments. Never do we see good works, in either Testament as criteria to earn God's favor. It is more likely Moses, Joshua, and all the Patriarchs were unwise and ignoble.

> "For you see your calling, brethren, that not many wise according to the flesh, not many mighty, not many noble, are called." 1Cor.1.26

> "The LORD did not set His love on you nor choose you because you were more in number than any other people, for you were the least of all peoples;" Deut.7:7

No one really knows which Pharaoh it was during the time of Joseph, or the accurate time of the Exodus for that matter. In the book of Exodus, the city of Raamses is referred to. But some scholars believe this reference was added to show geographically where the tribe of Israel lived but is supposed to be the most ancient Amarna, situated in the same area. Regardless of whether this theory is correct or not, the accurate picture of God was not actually represented until Jesus walked this earth. All other views of God were conclusions, perceived by what God had allegedly done through nature. For Israel, the process of maturing, and the gain of comprehending God, was a process of hundreds of years; and still, they had it so wrong, they did not recognize God or understand His voice, when He walked among them in the person of Jesus.

"Love suffers long and is kind; love does not envy; love does not parade itself, is not puffed up; does not behave rudely, does not seek its own, is not provoked, thinks no evil; does not rejoice in iniquity, but rejoices in the truth; bears all things, believes all things, hopes all things, endures all things. Love never fails. But whether there are prophecies, they will fail; whether there are tongues, they will cease; whether there is knowledge, it will vanish away. For we know in part and we prophesy in part. But when that which is perfect has come, then that which is in part will be done away. When I was a child, I spoke as a child, I understood as a child, I thought as a child; but when I became a man, I put away childish things. For now we see in a mirror, dimly, but then face to face. Now I know in part, but then I shall know just as I also am known. And now abide faith, hope, love, these three; but the greatest of these is love." 1Cor.13.4-13

Like myself, you have probably experienced a super abundance of love and mercy from God. What He does for us daily; how often He forgives us. The dramatic changes He's done in our hearts.

Whenever I have discussions with Christians, regardless of the variety, sooner or later the topic comes to our personal experience with God's goodness, He is good to all, despite the fact we deserve much less and continually fail.

When we read about love, how love *bears all things, believes all things, hopes all things, endures all things,* we don't often remember, these qualities apply to God for all mankind, because *He is* Love.

Evangelicals speak a lot about God's judgment, and how somehow God's anger and sense of justice must be appeased. Consequently, the secular world has a view of God inconsistent with the God most of us have experienced in Jesus. Yet, the Bible tells us, 'God is love.' It's almost as if we are speaking of two different Gods; the God of the Old Testament, and the one Jesus displayed.

Theologically, we know this cannot be; the thought is absurd. But reconciling our personal joy with God seems to conflict with what theologians tell us about Him.

Which are we to believe? Certainly, theological systems have answers to this, but I find their excuses for the God patterned after the Old Testament model to be unreasonable. They are as Spurgeon's: 'all these hard answers will come to us in eternity.'

I believe, in reality, His mercy is "from everlasting to everlasting." (Ps.103.17)

Could it be, theological systems and the beliefs of religious traditions fail to see God for who He really is? Could it be, modern religious systems which evolved through the Dark Ages, have us trapped by their skewed views; and now, like the Pharisees traditions, there is a disunion from what men say of God, and who He actually is?

If Jesus walked this earth today how would He look to us, would we recognize Him? But would He say to us, like He did Philip, 'Don't you know me Phil, haven't I been with you long enough for you to know who I am?' (Jn.14.9)

How did Philip picture God? No doubt he had an image in his mind about God, but it was so far off, he missed God when He was right in front of him.

I know this is hard for many of you reading this book. I just ask that you consider this logically:

What Greek manuscripts should we honor? Alternatively, one might ask, 'what manuscripts should we define as, 'The Word of God'?

You may say, "the whole Bible of course." Which Bible? No doubt you will answer according to the traditions of your church: Catholic = 73 books; Orthodox church = 77-81 (depending on the sect); Protestant church = 66 books. If you take the Protestant view; Martin Luther, the great hero of the Reformation, made his own list: The books of James, Hebrews, Jude and Revelation were omitted. According to Luther, these were not the 'Word of God.' He was also highly suspicious of 2Peter among other books. The 'Canon,' that group of books deemed God's word was voted on by a group of men; a committee. They had to sort through dozens of transcripts, all claiming to be Divinely inspired - God's Word.

Consider the times, peoples and the culture when these decisions were made. (Roughly 400 to 500 AD)

The same decisions were made, based on their view of God and life. Moreover, now you and today's Fundamentalist leaders pattern your life and theology on their conclusions!

Remember, unless you are Catholic or Orthodox, you probably would not appreciate the quality of religious worship going on in those days. These were no longer the pacifistic Christian disciples of Christ we see in the book of Acts. These were violent times and violent people. For instance, John of Nikiû an Egyptian Coptic Bishop from the 7th Century tells us:

> *"And, in those days, there appeared in Alexandria a female philosopher, a pagan named Hypatia, and she was devoted at all times to magic, astrolabes, and instruments of music, and she beguiled many people through Satanic wiles . . . A multitude of believers in God arose under the guidance of Peter the Magistrate . . . and they proceeded to seek for the pagan woman who had beguiled the people of the city and the Prefect through her enchantments. And when they learnt the place where she was, they proceeded to her and found her . . . they dragged her along till they brought her to the great church, named Caesareum. Now*

this was in the days of the fast. And they tore off her clothing and dragged her . . . through the streets of the city till she died. And they carried her to a place named Cinaron, and they burned her body with fire"

This confirmed what Socrates of Constantinople wrote, Socrates was a Christian historian and contemporary of Hypatia. (This is not Socrates, the famous Greek philosopher)

Even the most honored Christians during the time of deciding Canon had views ranging from 'odd,' to what some would call, heresy. Consider Augustine of Hippo, probably the most famous of the Church fathers (354-430) who had a huge influence on *Canon*. He believed:

- In using force against heretics, i.e. The **Donatists**

- Rituals of Baptism and the Lord's Supper were necessary for salvation.
- Did not believe in a literal reading of the Genesis creation story.
- Believed, Mary, mother of Jesus, was sinless and a perpetual virgin. (typical Catholic belief)
- That Hell was under the earth, and sinners suffered the fires of Hell in literal pain for eternity.

- Believed, it was sin to have sex with your wife unless to procreate.

I am not commenting on Augustine's beliefs; this is not my point. What I am trying to demonstrate is, during the time of the most monumental and significant decisions, on what constitutes "God's Word," the people who made these decisions, if polled, were just as diverse, odd, and inherently carnal as we are today. If you would read their arguments on the various books, excluded/included doctrines, you will see they argued, not necessarily under the anointing of the Holy Spirit, but according to popular tradition and their religious predispositions. Furthermore, to say their liturgical and cultural preferences did not affect their decisions is a fantasy.

All of the early Protestant teachers, Martin Luther, John Calvin, Erasmus, etc., were called "Reformers" because they had a significant history with the Catholic church, and in their minds 'The True Church' looked like the Catholic and Orthodox churches, but "reformed." There are those who believe King Henry VIII was a Reformer. John Calvin and Henry VIII, and many others were just as violent in heart, as the Popes, they were trying to bring down. Some condoning torture and murder to fight for their reformed beliefs. Few reformers understood the true Church, is in fact, invisible; and looks nothing like organized religion.

If you remember nothing else in this book; and disagree with its entire premise, I hope you will still agree with the following point:

If the history of Christianity interests you, like I, you have probably read volumes of books titled, "Church History." We have studied these books, took classes on the subject, taught on the topic of "Church History." As for me, for many years I was unaware I was not reading about 'The Church.' I was, in reality, reading about the struggle between three entities: "The Secular Government," "Organized Religion" and "The Church." Organized religion and The Church are entirely different entities.

However, there is an incredible mystery, some of us live in both of these entities at the same time. Moreover, a bigger mystery, most who do, do not know it?

The organized church has little to do with the Kingdom of God. It has as much to do with God's Kingdom as the folding chairs in the fellowship hall. However, of course, much grander in appearance.

Let us put this in perspective using someone like Augustine. Let us assume Augustine was indeed a Christian. Let's take away his robes. Let's remove from him all the tools of his trade; the sensors, the staff, any particular rings or ornaments that may distinguish him – take away all things that define him outwardly. Furthermore, let's take away the political power he had. Now we will remove him from his peers and magically transfer him to Papua New Guinea, and he finds himself sitting down with a single newly converted Christian. Now we have the Kingdom of God at its core; because Jesus will be there with them.

"For where two or three are gathered together in My name, I am there in the midst of them." Mat.18.20

If all things are as they should be, new believers will be added organically to their number; The Church will increase as the body exercises their gifts and they reach out to their neighbors. If they are meeting in a home, perhaps some more chairs are added. Being the more mature, Augustine will preach as he feels he should.

However, as soon as Augustine puts on a robe, or his chair is spray painted gold, suddenly the atmosphere changes. Augustine is no longer merely exercising his gift, but he is special; someone set apart, he feels it is his job. His robe confirms his position and status.

The longer Augustine is with this new tribe of believers, the more he remembers his traditions. He has within him a compulsion to set up regulations, rules, and finally catechisms to better define what it takes to be part of his group.

However, soon what Augustine brought with him, no longer looks like faith in Jesus, but faith in a system:

"making the word of God of no effect through your tradition which you have handed down. And many such things you do." Mk.7.13

God's pattern for the Church requires no holy objects in dress or furnishing of any kind. Regarding potential, no one is closer to God than any other. Because the Holy Spirit inhabits them, it is pre-assumed by the Apostles that every believer is part of a royal priesthood (1Pe.2.9).

Lost to many church organizations is the impact Jesus had on His disciples when He took a basin and a towel and washed their feet. This was not just an object lesson; this is how Jesus was. This is how all ministry should be approached; as Jesus said of Himself, '(I) came not to be served, but to serve' (Mat.20.28)

Aside from our differing gifts, the only real difference we have from one another is understanding God and His work; and our purpose, corporate and personal.

> *"Therefore let no one boast in men. For all things are yours: whether Paul or Apollos or Cephas, or the world or life or death, or things present or things to come– all are yours." 1Cor.3.21-22*

However, God being tolerant of men, He overlooks so much of the vanity of man's traditions and good intentions.

However, God's loving gaze is never on organizations. It is always on individuals. When He sees us, we are unclothed from our carnal administrations and the facade of our secondary identities. He sees us for what we are. He can sort us as only the Great Shepherd can. So collectively we are the Bride of Christ. Any administration which wanders from these facts is abandoning God's model for us. Also, if in any manner, we exclude a brother from fellowship, based on personal views of worship, however, lofty and high-sounding; thus making of him a second class citizen of the

Kingdom of God, we are in grave error, and reproaching Jesus, taking liberties with another person's servant.

> *"Let not him who eats **despise** him who does not eat, and let not him who does not eat judge him who eats; **for God has received him**. Who are you to judge another's servant? To his own master he stands or falls. Indeed, he will be made to stand, for God is able to make him stand."*
> *Rom.14.3-4*

Those who gave us the Bible were much like the Pharisee's in Paul's day. They were obsessed with politics, status, and their religious traditions. We cannot depend on a heightened measure of godliness to have guided them.

This does not mean God lost control. However, we must reform our definition of inspiration; God certainly was compelling His carnal children, but only in a manner similar to the way He compels kings or governments. Just enough inspiration, with a large measure of free will.

> *"The king's heart is in the hand of the LORD, Like the rivers of water; He turns it wherever He wishes."*
> *Prov.21.1*

Same Scripture, Different Views

Most of us believe what is popular in our Christian community; The New Testament Bereans give us an example how 'open-mindedness' can be part of culture. They are examples how we should treat all truth, traditional to our culture or not.

> *"These were more fair-minded than those in Thessalonica, in that they received the word with all readiness, and searched the Scriptures daily to find out whether these things were so". Act.17.11*

Are our personal feelings on doctrine a matter of human sentiment, or do they reflect the Holy Spirit residing in us? On the other side we could ask: Does what I believe reflect an honest view of scripture, or do my beliefs only reflect what my teachers have taught me? Either way, our subjective view of doctrine, or my predisposition to run with my peers are two human vulnerabilities we should be wary of.

Apparently, the Bereans were called more 'fair-minded,' or noble as the KJV translates, because the way they practiced their religion allowed them to be open minded to God's word, 'they received the word with all readiness.' Notice, the Bereans "received the word with all readiness," but then searched the scriptures to see if....". This demonstrates 'The Word' is somewhat different than the "scriptures." I'm am not saying there is always a hard distinction between the two, however, the message of the good news of Jesus, in the mouth of the disciples, was the "Word of God." And the scriptures, the Old Testament was used to confirm what the disciples proclaimed.

This brings an important question. In contrast, the Thessalonians were ignoble; apparently, the average Jew had a negative opinion of Jesus and "The Word" the disciples preached was considered heresy.

"But this I confess to you, that according to the Way which they call a sect (KJV 'heresy'), so I worship the God of my fathers, believing all things which are written in the Law and in the Prophets." Ac.24.14

Where then was the justification for the allegations of heresy? We see one doctrine repeatedly referred to in the New Testament, the Pharisees believed in the resurrection and afterlife, while the Sadducees, did not. This probably was not the point where the Bereans and the Thessalonians differed; as there were plenty of Pharisees who rejected Jesus as the Christ. And this begs the question, on what criteria were the early disciples "belief"- because the Jews and the followers of Jesus used the same 'Scriptures.' The difference may have been, how they viewed and discovered "the Word of God." If you have read any of my other writings, you might remember, it is believed there are 300+ prophecies concerning the coming Messiah in the Old Testament. I present a challenge to anyone 'to understand all 300 prophecies' without help from Bible commentators. Some are clear; many of these prophecies can be understood as local, and contemporary to the times they were declared. Some are so esoteric, one can only guess at their meaning. No wonder the majority of Jews missed who Jesus was. For The New Testament Church, the differences began with a revelatory understanding of the Old Testament, John the Baptist teaching and The Word he spoke concerning Jesus of Nazareth. The Word continued with the teachings of Jesus, then His disciples following Him. It is by these we know 'The Word of God' and understand prophecy.

Clearly, the Thessalonians had a difference of opinion than Paul about the promised Messiah. Does this make Paul a heretic? The Thessalonian's standard for 'believing 'the Law and Prophets' was different than Paul's statement to them. But there is something about meeting the Son of God which will alter everything you think you understand about God; this is what happened to Paul. When He and those who had a revelatory encounter with God, heard 'The Word,' the scriptures found their proper place. Suddenly a light shone from a different direction; things started to make sense. The Jews who didn't have ears to hear, or eyes to see, (Is.6.10) those in the old school, missed the Messiah. And are still in our world today, looking for a Messiah.

As I have already argued, the evangelical fundamentalist camp claim, "All the Bible is God's word." By insisting this doctrine, in a sense, they have sacrificed God's reputation for the sake of the doctrine of inerrancy.

It is one thing for churches to look utterly medieval. To claim the entire universe is only six or seven thousand years old; it is entirely another, to make God, who is Love, out to be Someone who is (apparently) arbitrary, and chooses some for eternal salvation, and others predestined to eternal damnation. And along with that, teaching that Joshua was only doing God's bidding while annihilating the lives of innocents.

Do we have a God who is entirely unreasonable? Or, could it be, man, who is fundamentally carnal, got some things wrong?

Just as this book contains errors in the text, grammar, and understanding, so also is anything man touches. As I said before, we leave an oily fingerprint on whatever we touch. This is true also of whatever man translates. All the translators of the Bible bring with them their own particular views.

No matter how much we try, we cannot escape who we are. We cannot, on command, be entirely objective. Any believer who has any experience with God working in his life knows that change comes incrementally.

I have no illusions that what I have written here will actually change minds. But what I hope is that my words will fan a spark of questions that are already there, and you will ask God to show you what is true.

There is a lot of, so called, science which cannot be proven, it is, therefore, theory. The big bang for instance, if God chose to create the universe in this way, because we are so far from the event, it impossible to prove. In like manner, the Bible stories are theory; and because much of what we believe is in this realm of theory, we must also use faith; Like scientists far from the big bang, we are physically far from the source of our inspiration. All we have are copies of copies of letters and stories. Compounded with that, are the multiple generations of cultures, entirely foreign to us, all standing between us and the events of the past. Whatever language Jesus spoke, Hebrew, Aramaic, Greek. Whatever the language of the original manuscripts, language has evolved and changed. Our English translations are a good example.

In the English language, there are many words which are archaic and meaningless to many today. For this reason (and others) the King James Bible is becoming less and less relevant. As examples:

- Choler - Anger, Dan.8.7

- Trow - Think or believe, Lu.17.9

- Bewrayeth - to show or make one visible, or apparent Pr.28.16

- Bolled - a bloomed Ex.9.31

There are several dozens of words in the old English Bible which almost no one uses today. This is how language, all languages, evolve.

Besides this, language is closely intertwined with culture. Without the cultural context, not only meanings for words, but the depth of understanding the heart of the speaker, is next to impossible. What follows is from one of the pages of the Summer Institute of Linguistics:

> *"On a practical level, language has to do with sounds, symbols and gestures that a community puts in order and associates so that they can communicate. On a deeper level, language is an expression of who we are as individuals, communities, nations. Culture refers to dynamic social systems and shared patterns of behavior, beliefs, knowledge, attitudes and values. Culture provides the environment in which languages develop, even as it influences how they are used and interpreted. For example, in many European cultures a "good day" is a sunny day, while in many African cultures a "good day" is a rainy day. Different culturally shared values provide the context for interpreting the term for "good".*

Besides the fact that Greek and Hebrew words can be translated into many English options, there are idioms and thoughts which are not translatable word for word. Compounding these problems are the preconceived notions of "Christian" translators. When the scripture is brought to us, tainting by the translators is indelibly imprinted upon the pages. This was particularly true for the older translations, before the science of translation had been developed. The worst offenders are those who carry with them doctrinal predispositions into their choice of words.

One example I often use has to do with the character of God, and how He is portrayed:

> *"And for this cause God shall send them strong delusion, that they should believe a lie: That they all might be **damned** who believed not the truth, but had pleasure in unrighteousness."* 2Th.2.11-12 *(King James Version)*

This example is particularly offensive to me as I can no longer abide anything close to sounding like the doctrine of 'Eternal Torment.' But putting my own prejudices aside, King James could have come up with something less severe.

Here are some of the other ways the King James version could have translated the Greek word 'Krino' (Damned): "avenge, conclude, condemn, decree, determine, esteem, judge, go to (sue at the) law, ordain, call in question, sentence to, think."

Context is a large factor in determining a translator's choice of words. Most newer translations use the word 'judged,' as with the New American Standard Bible:

> *"For this reason God will send upon them deluding influence so that they will believe what is false, in order that they all may be judged who did not believe the truth, but took pleasure in wickedness."* (NASB)

But *newer* does not always mean '*better*'. Here is the New King James Version, softened, but still Hell bent.

> *"And for this reason God will send them strong delusion, that they should believe the lie, that they all may be* **condemned** *who did not believe the truth but had pleasure in unrighteousness."* 2Th.2.11-12 (NKJV)

I hope this demonstrates my point. This book is not supposed to be an argument in favor or disfavor of particular translations. I will remind you, my hypothesis is to assert, 'that God uses carnal and vulnerable man to do His work on earth.' He has always done so, He always will. Finding the perfect Bible is like finding the proverbial 'perfect church'; as soon as you (or I) have a hand in it, it will no longer be perfect.

As I began this chapter, we are left with the stories of men just like us. But God is God, and He has not left us without help.

The Word of The Lord

Most Christians use *'The Word of God'* and *'The Scripture'* interchangeably; this is an error. And why? Because 'The Word of the Lord' is an utterance of God, and may develop a half-life as soon as men hear and repeat it. As in prophecy, God's Word may lay dormant for centuries, not finding any application until the right circumstances arise. Or His Word may have a single purpose, and have no further application.

On the other hand, 'the Scriptures' are a compilation of what men remember; and what they have surmised are God's Words, and His works among His people.

From the Scripture's collection to its translation, to its interpretation, textual analysis is a science, but it is not an exact science. For instance, since the Apostle Paul quoted from Isaiah, it is a safe bet the book of Isaiah came from Isaiah himself, and not a forgery. Also, scholars have excellent copies, which for the most part, agree with each other. With these analytics, and others, the book of Isaiah is deemed credible. But this says nothing about the manner in which Isaiah heard from God. It says nothing of his character. It says nothing about the quality of his walk with God. Things, if we were there, we probably could form an opinion, but still not tell with certainty. Neither can we say with absolute certainty, what the prophet said, has direct application to my circumstances. This takes, 'The Word of God'.

The Word of God is utterly perfect, but as I said, it's life is variable, and can be short, depending on God's intent. As a young believer, since I was told, "God's word will not return to Him void" (Is.55.11) I figured I should stand on the street corner and read and preach the Bible. "After all," I thought, "since God's Word always gives a return, the investment of my time will be rewarded by souls saved." The assumption is, we cannot lose if we only 'read God's Word' aloud to people.

In contrast, the book of Hebrews tells us:

"For the word of God is living and powerful, and sharper than any two-edged sword, piercing even to the division of soul and spirit, and of joints and marrow, and is a discerner of the thoughts and intents of the heart. And there is no creature hidden from His sight, but all things are naked and open to the eyes of Him to whom we must give account" Heb.4.12-13

Clearly, whoever wrote these words was not speaking of the Bible! The Bible cannot be called 'living.' Neither can the Bible 'discern'. And "all things are naked and open to, "the Bible's sight." I don't think so. No, "open to *His* sight." This is speaking about God This is not speaking of a document which has hundreds of thousands of variants. Try as we might, it is a great folly to call the Bible, God's Word.

The Bible is inspired, and the Bible contains records of God's Word, but most honest students of scripture cannot agree with many of the things attributed as God's commands. Oh yes, you may honestly believe it is God's Word. Moreover, as I pointed out earlier, you may agree with Charles Spurgeon's view, that such atrocity represents God's justice. However, your heart tells you otherwise. I have never met a Christian who did not recoil at the thought that God has something to do with all the atrocities recorded in Scripture. However, they just think, "These judgments seem extreme, but God must have had a good reason."

> *"O daughter of Babylon, who are to be destroyed, Happy the one who repays you as you have served us! Happy the one who takes and dashes Your little ones against the rock!" Ps.137.9*

Part of Spurgeon's commentary:

*"The murder of innocent infants can never be sufficiently deplored, but it was an incident of ancient warfare which the Babylonians had not omitted in their massacres, and, therefore, they were not spared it themselves. **The revenges of providence may be slow, but they are ever sure; neither can they be received with regret by those who see God's righteous hand in them**."*

If it were in any other context other than Christian and Jew, it is unlikely you would agree with that kind of justice. Most everyone reading this are as conflicted as I once was, because of the contrary nature of Jesus:

'Then Jesus said,

"Father, forgive them, for they do not know what they do." And they divided His garments and cast lots'. Lu.23.34

"Jesus Christ is the same yesterday, today, and forever." Heb.13.8

And why is it, as Spurgeon says, '... the murder of innocent infants can never be sufficiently deplored", yet he insists, 'this is part of God's justice.' When we assent to these stories as God's doing, we are not giving the benefit of the doubt to God, but are in reality, giving the benefit of the doubt to men who have ascribed this behavior to God. If we assent to something, which if in another context, we will condemn, is not the world correct when they say we are hypocrites? Can any reasonable mind settle this conflict? I tried for decades, and came to the conclusion, 'God is not like a man, no matter how much man attempts to make God in his image.'

The inspiration of Scripture is not, by necessity inerrant. The hundreds of thousands of variants are enough to prove this. For instance, as with the story I began with, I told you; "*God spoke to me and said, etc.*" This was over 30 years ago! God might have phrased His question to me in a manner different than I remember. Then if you were to repeat this story, you might further produce a *variant* of the facts. Nevertheless, the story is true. But more importantly, if I had included a hundred details (variants) which were wrong, the lesson would still be valid.

Tradition

As I have said, it is unlikely you would concur with the religious practices of those who first compiled the Bible; or even those who brought us our English translation. The Catholic and Orthodox institutions claimed to know God's mind, at the same time persecuted for centuries any who disagreed with their dogma. If you believe the application of their religious worship is faulty, why would you assume what they determined to be canon and translate is with perfection? Evangelical fundamentalists then tell us, 'well, it is not the copies which are perfect and inerrant, but the original manuscripts were perfect and inerrant". Then we must ask, 'why then make such a big deal about inerrancy if there is no definitive proof of it?" The implied answer we then receive; 'we will tell you what these copies mean; though the copies are imperfect, the doctrines based on them are.'

Must I submit my conscience to the views of another? Must I accept that God kills innocent children for the sake of the doctrine of 'inerrancy'?

As an alternative, if organized religion presents God to us in a manner inconsistent with the nature of Love, for God is Love, we should instead, side on love as our measure; and reject inferences which better describe the failings of man, than God.

What we have in the King James Version of the Bible, though from the church of England, is a heavily Catholic and cultural prejudice. Language reflect culture, and in this case, their skewed view of God. The Reformers were not exempt from this culture. In fact, John Calvin, one of the most famous reformers, continued with the pattern of persecution the Catholic institution so expertly developed. Moreover, Calvin, with his convoluted TULIP theory, made God into more of a monster than even the medieval Catholics could conceive. He did this with adjustments of words and ideas from scripture, to propose that God pre-ordains all men, to either an eternity in heaven or a hell of eternal suffering. This would be inconceivable to the Disciples who walked with the Prince of Peace, yet there are multitudes of Christians in the 21st century who honor John Calvin as the greatest theologian of all time!

Like the tool of money, God allows many carnal things to advance His Kingdom. Churches use lawyers, democracy, discipline, charters, membership, bylaws. We use gimmicks, fundraisers, pledges, to raise money. The larger churches use financial and growth consultants to help their growth. Furthermore, churches use hermeneutics, doctrinal schools, exegesis, apologetics, polemics, systematic theology, as an attempt to refine their doctrine.

Western churches in the modern age use all these things to advance the Kingdom of God, a Kingdom which is fundamentally spiritual in nature.

Because God continues to love and use carnal man, and does not thunder His disapproval from heaven against our methods, in our minds, God is endorsing our brand of Christianity. However, as God loved King David, a king with a type of government God did not want; still, He loves us and accepts most administrations of our choosing. However, just because God is tolerant of us, does not mean His endorsement.

Fundamentalism, because it sees every word of scripture as a declaration from heaven, it is inclined to understand scripture from a surface, exegetical point of view; as rules, ordinances, and commands. As an example: a friend of mine asked my opinion on a verse.

"The wife does not have authority over her own body, but the husband does. And likewise the husband does not have authority over his own body, but the wife does." 1Cor.7.4

He was having a disagreement with someone about the verse. My friend said, "I know what it says; I know what I've been taught what it means, but it doesn't set right with me".

I explained to him; this is because The Holy Spirit in him was fighting against the carnal and shallow approach of exegesis. It's entirely true each word in scripture can have a specific meaning, however, the spirit of the meaning is the 'Word of God- the Divine Expression.'

To understand what Paul was saying to the Corinthian church, one must first understand God's heart. This takes Paul's words out of the realm of instruction, and more into the realm of understanding and wisdom of how we should be servants to each other. So Paul's recommendation is no longer a recipe for a successful marriage; or a prescribed behavior for the marriage bed, but insight into God's heart. Paul was saying, how, even in the marriage bed, we are to forsake ourselves and serve the other. Where my friend was having an issue, was not the verse, but in the way he felt it was being represented.

How can any translation ever deal with such a thing as the marriage bed? Unbeliever and believers alike, often take exception to Paul's marriage counseling; and why? Because everything the carnal man defaults to, is a carnal and worldly approach. Paul, though unmarried, was qualified to teach about marriage because he understood the principles of the Kingdom of God. And since marriage is God's illustration of Jesus love for the Church, Paul's instruction was entirely consistent with God's Kingdom and its economy; whose currency is not money, but sacrificial love.

The Bible is full of this kind of wisdom. But understanding cannot always be found through exegesis; as Paul said:

"Now we have received, not the spirit of the world, but the Spirit who is from God, that we might know the things that have been freely given to us by God. These things we also speak, not in words which man's wisdom teaches but which the Holy Spirit teaches, comparing spiritual things with spiritual." 1Cor.2.12-13

As I have said, the Bible is not the Word of God, but the Word of God can be found there. It took inspiration to write the Bible, and because man touches the scripture, it takes inspiration to understand it. Since man has tampered with God's Word, in a sense, man has made it carnal. I do not mean this in the wicked sense because mankind cannot help but pollute what he touches. But God has given us a way, through the Holy Spirit, to understand God's ways and His work in the Church.

"But the natural man does not receive the things of the Spirit of God, for they are foolishness to him; nor can he know them, because they are spiritually discerned." 1Cor.2.14

Were Paul's instructions perfect, but he just didn't know it?

> *"A wife is bound by law as long as her husband lives; but if her husband dies, she is at liberty to be married to whom she wishes, only in the Lord. But she is happier if she remains as she is, according to my judgment–**and I think I also have the Spirit of God**. 1Cor.7.39-40*

Have you ever heard an inspired preacher? Is he 'inspired' 100% of the time? Apparently, Paul wasn't entirely sure when God was instructing by the Spirit, or these were thoughts through his own wisdom. How presumptuous he would have been had he believed, 'every word I speak is 'the Word of God.' We are just using speculation to think all the words recorded by every person in the Bible reflected God's heart.

As I have said, this cannot be, all men, but one, failed God. The shepherds of God's flock throughout Church history were just as vulnerable to wrong opinions as we are today.

"For we know that the law is spiritual, but I am carnal, sold under sin. For what I am doing, I do not understand. For what I will to do, that I do not practice; but what I hate, that I do. If, then, I do what I will not to do, I agree with the law that it is good. But now, it is no longer I who do it, but sin that dwells in me. For I know that in me (that is, in my flesh) nothing good dwells; for to will is present with me, but how to perform what is good I do not find. For the good that I will to do, I do not do; but the evil I will not to do, that I practice. Now if I do what I will not to do, it is no longer I who do it, but sin that dwells in me. I find then a law, that evil is present with me, the one who wills to do good. For I delight in the law of God according to the inward man. But I see another law in my members, warring against the law of my mind, and bringing me into captivity to the law of sin which is in my members. O wretched man that I am! Who will deliver me from this body of death? I thank God–through Jesus Christ our Lord! So then, with the mind I myself serve

the law of God, but with the flesh the law of sin."
Rom.7.14-25

The prevailing view of these verses is, Paul is stating the general spiritual condition of man, and victory is finally found in Romans chapter eight. This is certainly true, however, Paul is not speaking in the past tense, but in the present tense; indicating this is an ongoing struggle with Christians.

Furthermore, in contradiction to our 'positive confession' Christian brothers, Paul speaks of his own struggles:

*"For we do not want you to be ignorant, brethren, of our trouble which came to us in Asia: that **we were burdened beyond measure, above strength, so that we despaired even of life**. Yes, we had the sentence of death in ourselves, that we should not trust in ourselves but in God who raises the dead, 2Cor.1.8-9*

*"For indeed, when we came to Macedonia, our bodies had no rest, but we were troubled on every side. Outside were conflicts, **inside were fears**. **Nevertheless God, who comforts the***

downcast, comforted us *by the coming of Titus,"* 2Cor.7.5-6

Paul was confessing to being 'fearful and downcast'; our heroes in the faith were not perfect, but mere humans who experienced the same struggles we do today. It is an error to expect any more from the saints of the New Testament Church than we can accomplish through the same Holy Spirit in us. The only actual differences in their lives were their proximity in years to our Lord's ministry and the cultural appreciation for what He did and said.

Though Paul experienced similar passions as other men, even in the midst of his trials, he was still inspired. As we have already spoken, not with perfection, as his spirit still experienced enmity with his flesh. When we say a man is inspired, we cannot mean free from other influences. It is, therefore, with this caveat, as with 'the king's heart,' all men, including the most faithful, are ultimately still sovereign in their free will.

In contrast, this cannot be said of committees, or institutions. All corporate entities will ultimately exhibit more carnality, the more members there are. As I have previously stated, In the New Testament model, God has no relationship with institutions, only individuals.

The Unconditional Gift of The Holy Spirit

All Christian theologians agree, one does not have to be perfect to receive God. And all would agree, one does not have to be perfect to work for God. However, though God had a plan, Jonah demonstrates there are sometimes carnal causes for detours in God's plans. Yes, we know God is omniscient; He knows beforehand about the delays of His will. I suppose we can get ourselves all confused about the questions about God's "sovereignty" and His servants "freewill". But this just muddies the clear expressions and picture of the work of God's saints. Notice, The Apostle Paul didn't get all mixed up in theological, second guessing about God's predestination of Demas, when he lamented, "Demas has forsaken me, having loved this present world" (2Tim.4.10). I suppose Paul could have gone into a long diatribe how Demas wasn't part of the 'Elect.' No, the more obvious reason was simple, Demas found the world more attractive than ministry with the Apostle Paul. No doubt Demas was useful to ministry at one time, but now the cost to Demas was too high; his carnal side won out - God had called an imperfect vessel for

His work and for the time being, Demas was conflicted. This, as I have attempted to drive home, is the way it has always been.

When Paul said, 'no one stood with me,' I think he understood the vulnerabilities of men.

All throughout the epistles, Paul and the other Apostles were often writing about the common conditions of mankind in their times. Slavery and every kind of immorality were common; both around the world and in the Church. On top of this, continual persecution and every terror were a constant in the ancient world. The Church then had no other tools than we do today. Besides, we have the same Holy Spirit God has promised to all of His children.

The Need To Hear God

The institutions which gave us "The Bible" were administered with the same vulnerability as everything else man touches. The task of 'studying to show ourselves approved unto God' is a path congested with obstacles. We'd like to say, finding Christ's simplicity is easy, but the serpent continues his work.

> But I fear, lest by any means, as the serpent beguiled Eve through his subtilty, so your minds should be corrupted from the simplicity that is in Christ. 2Cor.11.3

For instance, prayer, we all wonder if we truly heard from God; "is that you God, or is that my mind playing tricks." We wonder this because our minds are not perfect, and our mind may be mixing what God is saying with our own thoughts. Everything we communicate about God, including the Bible, is filtered through the carnal minds of mankind.

Throughout Christian history, the sacred writings of godly men and women picked up a little of their carnal nature.

I hope this helps you see, the entire Bible was originally written, then transcribed, and translated with the most sincere and honest intentions, but man cannot easily escape the natural failings inherent in the flesh. It is, therefore, left to us to ask God for His heart on all the subjects and particulars of the Bible.

Not only in respect to the Bible but all of life. One of my first experiences after my wife and my conversions was facing a decision to follow our pastor and his flock into a Christian cult. At the time we had no idea where he was going, was a cult. We had no counsel except to follow him. Since we were brand new to such things, all discussions on the subject seemed legitimate. Why should we not follow the pastor we had grown to love? As it turned out, we did not follow him; and he wasted years before repenting of his decision. There is no accounting for our correct decision, except The Holy Spirit is especially gracious to the ignorant. Such guidance has been a constant throughout our lives. This is not to say, there have been no mistakes, no, but I can usually trace every false step to a problem with my carnal nature; pride, ambition, competition, arrogance; they all hide easily under the robes of the religious.

An Imperfect Bible, Then What?

Most Evangelical fundamentalists schools teach, "The Holy Spirit no longer reveals *The Word* in the same manner He did during the time of Christ and the early Church age." They say, "Since we have the perfect Bible, it has replaced all things supernatural." My writing is under the assumption that all believers have the Holy Spirit, as God gives Him, to anyone who asks. God gives His gifts willingly, regardless of our carnality, for it is the Holy Spirit who helps control our carnality.

> *"If you then, being evil, know how to give good gifts to your children, how much more will your heavenly Father give the Holy Spirit to those who ask Him!" Lu.11.13*

> *"But you are not in the flesh but in the Spirit, if indeed the Spirit of God dwells in you.* **Now if anyone does not have the Spirit of Christ, he is not His.***" Rom.8.9*

After we receive the Holy Spirit we can expect our new lives to be of a supernatural nature. This is why John could say:

> *"These things I have written to you concerning those who try to deceive you. But the anointing which you have received from Him abides in you, and you do not need that anyone teach you; but as the same anointing teaches you concerning all things, and is true, and is not a lie, and just as it has taught you, you will abide in Him." 1Jn.2.26-27*

John is describing a *supernatural* ability to discover those who might deceive us. This is a similar promise where Jesus promises the Holy Spirit's guidance to the disciples:

> *"But the Helper, the Holy Spirit, whom the Father will send in My name, He will teach you all things, and bring to your remembrance all things that I said to you." Jn.14.26*

Unquestionably we all get mixed up a bit. After decades of God leading me, I often get it wrong; and so do most Christians. However, there are those, again, who insist, 'there are no supernatural events in the

Church.' Oddly, these same people often declare things like, 'God called me into the ministry'; or 'God has led me to a larger church with more pay'; or, 'I felt God wanted me to pray for you.' All of these implying that somehow God is somehow communicating to them.

There is no scriptural evidence God no longer speaks to or inspires His people. The real reason dispensationalists insist God does not move Christians supernaturally through things like Prophecy, is because of fear. Church leaders are afraid of people going off the deep end, or afraid pastors will lose control of the worship service to people believing God can speak through them. Consequently, large portions of the chapters of 1 Corinthians 12 and 14 are considered invalid or no longer relevant.

Yes, there is no shortage of real oddballs in the Church. And many who say, 'God has spoken' to them. However, Paul in 1Cor.14.29, indicates this is an acceptable risk. Apparently, Paul believed the Church would be enriched by the average Christian expressing his or her gift.

"Let two or three prophets speak, and let the others judge. But if anything is revealed to another who sits by, let the first keep silent. For you can all

prophesy one by one, that all may learn and all may be encouraged." 1Cor.14.29-31

Many schools of thought do not believe this, but they have a problem. These same schools of usually think that the Bible is perfect and thorough. Can you see the issue here? As quoted, John tells us (1Jn.2.27) The Holy Spirit will lead us into all truth, yet this school of thought teaches the Holy Spirit is no longer active in this way. How can the scripture be thorough, and "that which is perfect" which was to come (1Cor.13.10) be telling us the opposite of what John speaks 'in the perfect Bible? This makes no sense.

I need to say one more point on this. The supernatural gifts of the Spirit do not have to be the spooky, voodoo type things like you see in so many churches. I remember as a child when escaping the cold; I walked into a church. What I saw was the chaos of people writhing on the floor, shouting unintelligibly. Also, I am not saying God does not accept this as worship; I am saying, things esoteric does not have to be chaotic or mystical looking for it to be a genuine move of God's Spirit. Prophecy need not sound like anything other than simple forth-telling, or regular preaching.

Anointed prayer and words of knowledge (1Cor.12.8) do not need to sound bombastic or aggressive to be admonitions from God; any more than a missionary needs to dress in drab colors or continually wear a solemn face to be effective.

The Spirit-controlled life and the expression of one's gift should be as natural for the Christian as a mother attends sweetly and lovingly to her child. The Spirit-controlled Christian is essentially a life sensitive to both God's heart and the needs of those around them.

On the other hand, some are afraid of all emotion in their faith. How would it be if our family life were void of all expressions of emotion? Can parenting be truly successful if the child feels no love for it? When we pray, should we not do so with passion? Jesus prayed earnestly with cries and tears (Heb.5.7) Paul and Silas sang psalms and hymns of praise (Ac.16.25) Were these dry readings and monotones of only the psalmist's expressions, or were they heartfelt?

There are thousands of references to prayer throughout the scriptures. At the very least, prayer is an attempt at the supernatural; a connection to God. It is the extension of that part of our faith, where we believe He is, and He rewards our communications with Him.

Final Thoughts

I have established how the stories of the Bible was lived and recorded, translated, and interpreted by carnal men. It is impossible that carnal men or women can fully understand the Logos, except as seen through the person of Jesus – The Word of God (Jn.1.1-14). Though He is God in the flesh, He is the only non-carnally minded, sinless, and unbiased representation of God.

What I believe to be the Word of God in Scripture, must align with the Personification of Jesus as the Holy Spirit has shown Him to me. This is faith:

"For Moses writes about the righteousness which is of the law, "The man who does those things shall live by them. But the righteousness of faith speaks in this way, "Do not say in your heart, 'Who will ascend into heaven?' " (that is, to bring Christ down from above) or, " 'Who will descend into the abyss?' " (that is, to bring Christ up from the dead). But what does it say? "The word is near you, in your mouth and in your heart" (that is, the word of faith which we preach): that if you confess with your mouth the Lord Jesus and *believe in your heart that God has raised Him from the dead, you will be saved." Rom.10.5-9*

The meaning of this verse, I think, is simple; We cannot bring Jesus down from heaven to know Him, neither can we descend to the abyss and discover about Him there. However, we are not without hope in finding Him! "The Word is near you, even in your heart."

Please, please do not only depend on men to tell you how to find God, or to discover who He is; 'The Word' is already near you, even in your heart." You hold within your heart the very tools which can define the Truth; trust what He has done for you.

Finally, if you have read this far, you may have been challenged into reconsidering the scriptures as inerrant. I hope you notice; I am not attacking the belief that God has given us the Bible; I am only demonstrating two things: Inerrancy cannot be true, and we cannot place our faith in anything other than God. The Bible is full of wisdom, insight, and instruction. It is a lamp for our feet as we walk through life. We will never exhaust the treasures God has placed there for us. However, God's treasure is not for the heartless, lazy, or passively religious, it must be mined:

"Yes, if you cry out for discernment, And lift up your voice for understanding, If you seek her as silver, And search for her as for hidden treasures; Then you will understand the fear of the LORD, And find the knowledge of God. For the LORD gives wisdom; From His mouth come knowledge and understanding" Pr.2.4-6

I have found when I suggest the Bible has errors; the hearers react as if I am taking away every support and security of their faith. I suppose for some, I am. This begs the question, 'should the Christian's security be in something which has been overly administered by man? In my mind, this type of security is misplaced. Imagine you are hiking a mountain ridge of solid and stable rock ten foot wide, and this ridge goes straight up the mountain to the top. The name of this ridge is, 'Love God with all your heart.' On both sides left and right the precipice falls hundreds of feet. If you fell, you would certainly experience death. This ridge is part of the beauty of the mountain, but some well-meaning soul decided to install a handrail on both sides of the ridge.

This handrail can represent our belief that the stories of the Bible are, in every sense, historically correct and represent God's true nature; and it is a perfect document. For goodness sake, the ridge is ten foot wide; if the handrail is taken away, simply stay close to the center of the ridge, and you will be fine!

If you have indeed fallen in love with God; if it is Him you have a relationship with; and not just a book, or denomination, or a school of thought, the absence of the handrail - the belief the Bible is inerrant, is not necessary.

I hope you see; the handrail was added as a means of control; for fear you may step off the precipice into unbelief. So I ask you, what is your faith in? Is it in God's love for you, and our Rock Jesus? Alternatively, is your faith in the handrail?

*"He who believes in the Son of God **has the witness in himself**; he who does not believe God has made Him a liar, because he has not believed the testimony that God has given of His Son." 1Jn.5.10*

"There is no fear in love; but perfect love casts out fear, because fear involves torment. But he who fears has not been made perfect in love." 1Jn.4.18

Q-1. *It sounds like your brand of Christianity is entirely subjective. What if you are wrong about what you think you believe?*

A. Whenever we speak of anything that is fundamentally supernatural; where there is some esoteric connection with an invisible God, our experience is always subjective. If that connection you and I claim to have, does not exist, then we have larger problems than our view of scripture. However, if that connection exists, then the promises of 1Jn.2.27 are in effect. That is God's promise.

Q-2. *My Pastor says, 'when the canon was decided God ceased using the miraculous'. Why should I believe you that he is wrong?*

A. He and I get our information from the same Bible. It is likely he has a schooled interpretation of 1Cor.13.8 to justify his position. In fact, he must use, what's called *eisegesis* to make this claim. I think you should trick him. Before asking him about 1Cor.13.8...Ask him, *'Pastor, what do you think of eisegesis?'* Likely he will hate it. This will demonstrate he is schooled, and not objective about the topic.

Q-3 *Virtually all secular Egyptologists believe the Exodus never happened. Their finding also show, ' outside the Bible, there is no definitive records of Israel in Egypt; and no record of the conquests of Canaan.' Are you aligning yourself with that view?*

A. No, I do not agree with that view. I believe Israel had a history of Egypt and Canaan, but I also believe most Bible scholars and Egyptologists have the timing wrong. However, I do believe some of the histories of the Old Testament records were 'doctored'; to make Israel larger than they were. However, if my hypothesis is correct, and ancient Israel misrepresented our God of love, "doctoring the records", is in comparison, trivial.

Q-4 *You seem to have no confidence in Scripture, yet you use Scripture throughout your book; is that not speaking out of both sides of your mouth?*

A. This is an easy question in one sense; while hard in another. Believing the Bible is inerrant would require you to stone your kids when they are stubborn and rebellious (Duet.21.18-21.)

I am unconcerned with obviously barbaric views some of the old commandments demonstrate. Some scriptures are harder. However, Paul said, Christ took the 'requirements/ordinances contrary to us, nailing them to the cross' (Col.2.14) This does not mean these ordinances were, in fact, from God. It follows, these were attempts to make themselves right before God, believing this was God's desire.

All that said, I want to believe the entirety of the Bible is true, but whenever the Bible obviously conflicts with reason or violates God's default quality- love, God's reputation always wins out for me. Therefore, in my view, I worshiping God, not the Bible.

Q-5 *You say Jesus should be the stumbling stone and not Christians. However, didn't Jesus say, 'if they hate me, they will hate you.'*

A. Yes, we can expect to be hated of all nations; but this should not be because of the Bible's representation of God. It should be because we are the light, as Jesus was light, we also expose darkness by our lives. (Jn.3.19)

Sadly, what has happened, is mankind hates the organized church. The organized church can be overtly worldly, corrupt, arrogant and introverted. Naturally, man sees churches as irrelevant to their lives.

It is possible, however, not to be in the culture of Christianity, yet love, and have faith in and follow Jesus without all the cultural baggage.

Q-6 *You quoted the Apostle Paul when he said to Felix; 'I believe all the law and prophets' (Ac.24.14). Do you not believe 'the law and prophets,' like Paul?*

A. As I said in my book, 'Traversing Babylon,' I believe the moral lessons of the Old Testament, but I do not necessarily believe everything represented as fact. However, isn't this the point of the Bible; to teach us the meaning and the lessons of God's central points? For instance, we are told, 'a serpent deceived Eve.' If we get into arguments whether, at one time or another, there were talking snakes, isn't that distracting and beside the point? This could be an indicator if your faith is in God or the facts of Bible. What if you should find there never have been talking serpents, where now do you find your faith? Regardless, if there were talking snakes or not, the lessons of the story are still true.

Q-7 *Your book cover is terribly graphic. It appears more like a book cover for religious extremism. Do you think this is appropriate for a Christian book?*

A. Yes, it is graphic. The story of David and Goliath is a standard curriculum for small children in Sunday

Schools. The cover is designed to help us realize what these cultures were like, and cause us to question how much they were able to define and represent God.

Made in the USA
Middletown, DE
26 September 2016